How to Raise and Train an
AFGHAN

By SUNNY SHAY
and SARA M. BARBARESI

Distributed in the U.S.A. by T.F.H. Publications, Inc., 211 West Sylvania Avenue, P.O. Box 27, Neptune City, N.J. 07753; in England by T.F.H. (Gt. Britain) Ltd., 13 Nutley Lane, Reigate, Surrey; in Canada to the book store and library trade by Clarke, Irwin & Company, Clarwin House, 791 St. Clair Avenue West, Toronto 10, Ontario; in Canada to the pet trade by Rolf C. Hagen Ltd., 3225 Sartelon Street, Montreal 382, Quebec; in Southeast Asia by Y.W. Ong, 9 Lorong 36 Geylang, Singapore 14; in Australia and the south Pacific by Pet Imports Pty. Ltd., P.O. Box 149, Brookvale 2100, N.S.W., Australia. Published by T.F.H. Publications, Inc. Ltd., The British Crown Crown Colony of Hong Kong.

Mr. George Pickow of Three Lions, Inc. was assigned to photograph the Afghans at Grandeur Kennels , 302 West John Street, Hicksville, New York. (He was so impressed with the dogs that he obtained one for his family from Mrs. Sunny Shay, owner of the kennels.)

ISBN 0-87666-232-7

Library of Congress Catalog Card No. 57-13283
© Copyright, 1958

Contents

The desirable Afghan type in three colors. These dogs show the keen look of the Eastern hunter.

1. Afghan Hound Standards

Called the "dog of Noah's Ark" by tribesmen hunters of Afghanistan, the Afghan Hound is probably the most ancient of breeds. With his proud carriage, regal action and flowing coat and topknot, he is also one of the most unusual dogs in appearance, sure to attract attention wherever he goes.

Although the Afghan is a newcomer to America, having been here only about thirty years, his colorful history goes back an estimated 8,000 years. The actual age of the breed is a disputed point, but all acknowledge it to be the oldest of known breeds. Long-haired dogs of the greyhound type were pictured and described in Egypt of 4000 B.C. The royal rulers took great pride in their hunting dogs and would keep only the best. So it came about that Afghans earned royal favor and were kept in packs for hunting. They were often the pampered pets of royal princesses and became known as the dogs of royalty; they are still called that today.

Afghans were jealously guarded and great care was taken in the breeding and pedigree records. At times one royal household might present a gift of a fine hound to another as a token of friendship. This may have been the way in which, during succeeding centuries, they arrived in Afghanistan, the rugged, mountainous country which gives the breed its name.

The Afghan has been put to a wide variety of uses down through the centuries, always living close to men. His reputation as a hunter is unexcelled in his native land where he has been used against a variety of wild game, including antelope and gazelle and even the dangerous snow leopard. Hunting in packs, Afghans work in pairs to bring down their prey, although noted hunters are credited with kills singlehanded. The Afghan possesses great speed and stamina and can travel over rocky, rugged ground with ease, due to his unique structure. The Afghan's wide, high hip bones are found in no other breed, and this prominence gives puppies particularly a gaunt look. The huge paws, well protected by heavy hair between the pads, give an Afghan good footing on rough terrain.

The Afghan's long legs and deep chest also come from ancestors selected for their ability to twist and turn and leap over obstacles in pursuit of game. The powerful jaw and well-muscled frame were needed for a dog to pull down such prey as the fierce wildcats.

The Afghan has many capabilities. In his native country, his herding instinct has been put to use on flocks of sheep and goats. There has also

Teach your puppy to pose on a bench while he is still young, to prepare him for show days ahead. This Afghan puppy's coat is still short

been some interest in racing. Some served in World War II as sentry and messenger dogs, not a new use as Afghans often served as war dogs. An oft-told tale concerns the pack of hounds which guarded the British military post at Chaman, India. Fed by the soldiers but otherwise untrained for the duty, and wild, they assumed responsibility for guarding the post by night, some standing with the sentries and others patrolling in pairs around the walls.

As a rare breed, the Afghan has had fewer opportunities than other breeds to prove his worth, but he has gained respect in many fields. The Afghan is dignified and aloof, although puppies are as clownish and frolicsome as any. His air of keen fierceness may awe those who do not know the breed. In spite of the Afghan's appearance of looking "at and through one" (as the English standard described the desirable expression), no dog is more devoted to his master nor is a better family companion and guardian.

The first Afghans known in the West came to England in the 1890's, and it was not until the 1920's that the breed began to be popular; ten years later it first appeared in America. Since then, however, it has been a rising star of the dog world—over halfway up the scale of popularity. There are more than 4,000 in the United States today.

Also called the Balkh, Barakzai and Kurram Valley Hound, after the particular region where the finest specimens were found, the Afghan is adapted by that violent climate to living in any environment, hot or cold. Called "monkey-faced hound" because of his appealing face, the Afghan shows in build his close relationship to other sight hounds (dogs which hunt primarily by sight rather than scent) of the Near East: the Saluki, Russian Wolfhound, Greyhound, and smaller Whippet.

Another appropriate name is "Cowboy Dog," because of the shaggy, chap-like hair on the legs. His long coat adds grace to the Afghan, but it is no nuisance; hardly any hair is shed, and an occasional brushing keeps it in order.

The distinctive Afghan is suitable for both city and country life. Although capable of great speed and endurance in the field, and a keen and clever hunter, the Afghan is content to lead the quiet life of the city dog, taking his daily constitutional with much dignity. Well-mannered and gentle, with classic beauty, he is accepted in the best of company. Afghans are very quiet, seldom barking unless it is necessary. Although a rugged individualist, the Afghan is blessed with a high degree of intelligence and is readily trained. He is quick to learn and eager to please a master he loves. Afghans are extremely gentle with children and small animals. It is a sight to see one playing with a cat or kitten, sometimes carrying it in his mouth with the same gentle manner as a cat carrying her babies. They are naturals as children's playmates and guardians, very possessive about homes and families. Even though reserved with strangers, the Afghan is a great clown, never seems to grow up, and provides great entertainment for his family. He is an amusing and interesting all-around companion. His exotic appearance has inspired poets: the fine, silky coat, topknot shading the far-seeing Oriental eyes, graceful lines of the body, odd, ringed tail. Here, indeed, is something different, a dog of which you can be proud.

The Afghan hound is available in a variety of colors to please many tastes. Most often seen are cream, fawn, red, and black. More rare are the black-and-tan, various brindles and greys, blues and silvers. Although many people think of the Afghan complete with black mask and ear tips, these are not always found, and are not at all necessary.

KENNEL CLUB SPECIFICATIONS

Here are the standards by which the Afghan is judged, drawn up by the Afghan Hound Club of America (founded 1935), Mrs. D. R. Carlsen, secretary, 144 Columbia Road, Ellicott City, Maryland; and approved by the Board of Directors of the American Kennel Club, 221 Fourth Avenue, New York City.

GENERAL APPEARANCE: The Afghan Hound is an aristocrat, his whole appearance one of dignity and aloofness with no trace of plainness or coarseness. He has a straight front, proudly carried head, eyes gazing into the distance as if in memory of ages past. The striking characteristics of the breed—exotic or "Eastern" expression, long silky topknot, peculiar coat pattern, very prominent hip bones, large feet, and the impression of a somewhat exaggerated bend in the stifle due to profuse trouserings—stand out clearly giving the Afghan Hound the appearance of what he is, a King of Dogs, that has held true to tradition throughout the ages.

HEAD: The head is of good length showing much refinement, the skull evenly balanced with the foreface. There is a slight prominence of the nasal bone structure causing a slightly Roman appearance, the center line running up over the foreface with little or no stop, falling away in front of the eyes so there is an absolutely clear outlook with no interference; the underjaw showing great strength, the jaws long and punishing; the mouth level, meaning that the teeth from the upper jaw and lower jaw match evenly, neither overshot nor undershot. (This is a difficult mouth to breed. A scissors bite is even more punishing and can be more easily bred into a dog than a level mouth, and a dog having a scissors bite, where the lower teeth slip inside and rest against the teeth of the upper jaw, should not be penalized.) The occipital bone is very prominent. The head is surmounted by a topknot of long, silky hair.

EARS: The ears are long, set approximately on level with outer corners of the eyes, the leather of the ear reaching nearly to the end of the dog's nose, and covered with long, silky hair.

EYES: The eyes are almond shaped (almost triangular), never full or bulgy, and they are dark in color.

NOSE: The nose is of good size, black in color.

HEAD FAULTS: Coarseness; snipiness; overshot or undershot; eyes round or bulgy or light in color; exaggerated Roman nose; head not surmounted with topknot.

NECK: The neck is of good length, strong and arched, running in a curve to the shoulders which are long and sloping and well laid back. FAULTS: Neck too short or too thick; a ewe neck; a goose neck; a neck lacking substance.

BODY: The back line appears practically level from the shoulders to the loin; strong and powerful loin and slightly arched, falling away toward the stern, with the hip bones very pronounced; well ribbed and tucked up in flanks. The height at the shoulders equals the distance from the chest to

Two or more Afghans will get along well together. Usually they are quiet and gentle, although they will often enjoy a romp with their owner.

the buttocks; the brisket well let down and of medium width. FAULTS: Roach back; sway back; goose rump; slack loin; lack of prominence of hip bones; too much width of brisket causing interference with elbows.

9

TAIL: The tail is set not too high on the body, having a ring or a curve on the end. It should never be curled over, or rest on the back, or be carried sideways, and is never bushy.

LEGS: The forelegs are straight and strong with great length between elbow and pastern; elbows well held in; forefeet large in both length and width; toes well arched; feet covered with long, thick hair, fine in texture; pasterns long and straight; pads of feet unusually large and well down on the ground. Shoulders have plenty of angulation so that the legs are well set underneath the dog. Too much straightness of shoulder causes the dog to break down in the pasterns, and this is a serious fault.

All four feet of the Afghan Hound are in line with the body, turning neither in nor out. The hind feet are broad and of good length; the toes arched, and covered with long, thick hair; hindquarters powerful and well muscled with great length between hip and hock; hocks are well let down; good angulation of both stifle and hock; slightly bowed from hock to crotch. FAULTS: Front or back feet thrown outward or inward; pads of feet not thick enough; feet too small; or any other evidence of weakness in the feet; weak or broken down pasterns; too straight in stifle; too long in hock.

COAT: Hindquarters, flanks, ribs, forequarters, and legs are well covered with thick, silky hair, very fine in texture; ears and all four feet well feathered. From in front of the shoulders and also backwards from the shoulders along the saddle from the flanks and ribs upwards, the hair is short and close, forming a smooth back in mature dogs—this is a traditional characteristic of the Afghan Hound.

The Afghan Hound is shown in its natural state; the coat is not clipped or trimmed; the head is surmounted (in the full sense of the word) with a topknot of long, silky hair. Showing of short hair on cuffs on either front or back legs is permissible. FAULTS: Lack of short-haired saddle in mature dogs.

HEIGHT: Dogs, 27 inches, plus or minus one inch. Bitches, 25 inches, plus or minus one inch.

WEIGHT: Dogs, about sixty pounds. Bitches, about fifty pounds.

COLOR: All colors are permissible, but color or color combinations are pleasing. White markings, especially on the head, are undesirable.

GAIT: When running free, the Afghan Hound moves at a gallop, showing great elasticity and spring in his smooth, powerful stride.

When on a loose lead, the Afghan can trot at a fast pace. Stepping along, he has the appearance of placing the hind feet directly in the footprints of the front feet, both thrown straight ahead. Moving with head and tail high, the whole appearance of the Afghan Hound is one of great style and beauty.

TEMPERAMENT: Aloof and dignified, yet gay. FAULTS: Sharpness or shyness.

2. Buying Your Afghan

Perhaps you decided that you want an Afghan Hound after seeing one of this elegant, impressive breed. Now that you have decided on an Afghan, it is time to go about getting him—or her.

First, make up your mind what you want: male or female, adult or puppy, show dog or "just a pet." There is no greater use for a dog than being "just" a beloved pet and companion, but the dog which has profitable show and breeding possibilities is worth more to the seller.

PET OR SHOW DOG?

The puppy with a slight flaw in his ear carriage or quantity of coat will make just as good a companion and guardian, but his more perfect litter mate will cost more.

That is why there is often a difference in price between puppies which look—to you, anyway—identical. If you think you may want to show your dog or raise a litter of puppies for the fun of it later on, by all means buy the best you can afford. You will save expense and disappointment later on. However, if the puppy is *strictly* a pet for the children, or companion for you, you can afford to look for a bargain. The pup which is not show material; the older pup, for which there is often less demand; or the grown dog, not up to being used for breeding, are occasionally available and are opportunities to save money. Remember that these are the only real bargains in buying a dog. It takes good food and care—and plenty of both—to raise a healthy, vigorous puppy.

The price you pay for your dog is little compared to the love and devotion he will return over the many years he'll be with you. With good care and affection your pup should live to a ripe old age; through modern veterinary science and nutrition, dogs are better cared for and living longer. The average life expectancy of this long-lived breed is twelve years, and dogs in their teens are not uncommon.

MALE OR FEMALE?

If you should intend breeding your dog in the future, by all means buy a female. You can find a suitable mate without difficulty when the time comes, and have the pleasure of raising a litter of pups—there is nothing cuter than a fat, playful puppy. If you don't want to raise puppies, your female can be spayed, and will remain a healthy, lively pet. The female is smaller than the male and generally quieter. She has less tendency to roam in search of romance, but a properly trained male can be a charming pet, and has a certain difference in temperament that is appealing to many people. Male vs. female is chiefly a matter of personal choice.

ADULT OR PUP?

Whether to buy a grown dog or a small puppy is another question. It is undeniably fun to watch your dog grow all the way from a baby, sprawling and playful, to a mature, dignified dog. If you don't have the time to spend on the more frequent meals, housebreaking, and other training a puppy needs in order to become a dog you can be proud of, then choose an older, partly trained pup or a grown dog. If you want a show dog, remember that no one, not even an expert, can predict with 100% accuracy what a small puppy will be when he grows up. He may be right *most* of the time, but six months is the earliest age for the would-be exhibitor to pick a prospect and know that his future is relatively safe.

If you have a small child it is best to get a puppy big enough to defend himself, one not less than four or five months old. Older children will enjoy playing with and helping to take care of a baby pup, but at less than four months a puppy wants to do little but eat and sleep, and he must be protected from teasing and overtiring. You cannot expect a very young child to understand that a puppy is a fragile living being; to the youngster he is a toy like his stuffed dog.

WHERE TO BUY

You can choose among several places to buy your dog. One is a kennel which breeds show dogs as a business and has extra pups for sale as pets. Another is the one-dog owner who wants to sell the puppies from an occasional litter, paying for the expenses being his chief aim. Pet shops usually buy puppies from overstocked kennels or part-time hobbyists for re-sale, and you can generally buy a puppy there at a reasonable price. To find any of these, watch the pet column of your local newspaper or look in the classified section of your phone book. If you or your friends go driving out in the countryside, be on the lookout for a sign announcing pure-bred puppies for sale.

Whichever source you try, you can usually tell in a very short time whether the puppies will make healthy and happy pets. If they are clean,

Any one of these puppies would make a handsome and lovable pet to take home.

fat and lively, they are probably in good health. At the breeder's you will have the advantage of seeing the puppies' mother and perhaps the father and other relatives. Remember that the mother, having just raised a demanding family, won't be looking her best, but if she is sturdy, friendly and well-mannered, her puppies should be, too. If you feel that something is lacking in the care or condition of the dogs, it is better to look elsewhere than to buy hastily and regret it afterward.

You may be impatient to bring home your new dog, but a few days will make little difference in his life with you. Often it is a good idea to choose a puppy and put a deposit on him, but wait to take him home until you have prepared for the new arrival. For instance, it is better for the Christmas puppy to be settled in his new home before the holidays, or else to wait until things have settled down afterward. You may want to wait until the puppy has completed his "shots," and if this is arranged in advance, it is generally agreeable.

If you cannot find the dog you want locally, write to the secretary of the A.K.C. (page 16), for names of breeders near you, or to whom you can write for information. Puppies are often bought by mail from reputable breeders.

WHAT TO LOOK FOR IN A PUPPY

In choosing your puppy, assuming that it comes from healthy, well-bred parents, look for one that is friendly and out-going. The biggest pup in the litter is apt to be somewhat coarse as a grown dog, while the appealing "poor little runt" may turn out to be a timid shadow—or have a Napoleon complex! If you want a show dog and have no experience in choosing the prospect, study the standard (page 8), but be advised by the breeder on the finer points of conformation. His prices will be in accord with the puppies' expected worth, and he will be honest with you because it is to his own advantage. He wants his good puppies placed in the public eye to reflect glory on him—and to attract future buyers.

You'll be quite surprised on seeing your first Afghan puppy; he will look little like the adult. He will have a short coat which begins to grow in puppyhood and continues until maturity. By 16 or 18 months it becomes apparent that the puppy will look like an Afghan. Afghan puppies are thinner than other breeds, with prominent hip bones protruding and long gangly legs which make them appear colt-like, and this is the Afghan puppy's charm.

At first the muzzle is rather blunt, but it will eventually lengthen and chisel correctly. The puppy should have a bright eye, with no mattering in the corner. The eyes should be small and dark, the head well balanced, with no thickness or coarseness in the skull, ears low set and well coated. The nose should be black, although liver is permitted in a light-colored dog. The neck, of great length, is strong and arched, the chest deep, and back quite straight. The forelegs should be straight. The feet, which are large in the adult, will appear ridiculously big in the puppy. The hindquarters are powerful and hind legs very long between the hip and hock (or heel) joint; short from there to the ground.

The puppy's coat will not be evident until about five months, so the puppy will appear even more gangling, and the hip bones should be prominent. The tail is set on low with a ring at the end, and is carried high when the dog is in motion. Although the puppy is awkward and gawky, he should give promise of great reach of angulation and style in motion.

Now that you have paid your money and made your choice, you are ready to depart with puppy, papers and instructions. Make sure that you know his feeding routine, and take along some of the food. It is best to make any diet changes gradually so as not to upset his digestion. If the puppy is not fed before leaving he will ride comfortably on your lap where he can see out of the window. Take along a rag or newspapers for accidents.

His grin shows how delighted this boy is with his Afghan puppy. Note that he is carrying the puppy the right way so that he can not fall or get hurt, although the Afghan looks like a colt with his lanky legs hanging down.

PEDIGREES

When you buy your puppy you should receive his pedigree and registration certificate or application. These have nothing to do with licensing, which is a local regulation applying to pure-bred and mongrel alike. Find out the local ordinance in regard to age, etc., buy a license, and keep it on your dog whenever he is off your property.

Your dog's pedigree is a chart, for your information only, showing his ancestry. It is not part of his official papers. The registration certificate is the important part. If the dog was named and registered by his breeders you will want to complete the transfer and send it, with the fee of $1.00, to the American Kennel Club, 221 Fourth Ave., New York 3, N. Y. They will transfer the dog to your ownership in their records, and send a new certificate to you.

If you receive instead, an application for registration, you should fill it out, choosing a name for your pup, and mail it with the fee of $2.00 to the A.K.C. Be sure that the number of the puppy's litter is included.

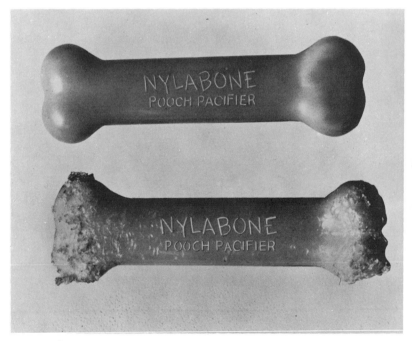

NYLABONE® is a necessity that is available at your local petshop (not in supermarkets). The puppy or grown dog chews the hambone flavored nylon into a frilly dog toothbrush, massaging his gums and cleaning his teeth as he plays. Veterinarians highly recommend this product . . . but beware of cheap imitations which might splinter or break.

This dog is Ch. Shirkhan of Grandeur, Best in Show at Westminster, 1957

3. Care of the Afghan Puppy

BRINGING YOUR PUPPY HOME

When you bring your puppy home, remember that he is used to the peace and relative calm of a life of sleeping, eating and playing with his brothers and sisters. The trip away from all this is an adventure in itself, and so is adapting to a new home. So let him take it easy for awhile. Don't let the whole neighborhood pat and poke him at one time. Be particularly careful when children want to handle him, for they cannot understand the difference between a delicate living puppy and the toy dog they play with and maul. If the puppy is to grow up loving children and taking care of them, he must not get a bad first impression.

FEEDING YOUR PUPPY

It is best to use the feeding schedule to which the puppy is accustomed, and stick to it except when you feel you can modify or improve it. You will probably want to feed the puppy on one of the commercially prepared dog foods as a base, flavoring it with table scraps and probably a little meat and fat when you have them. Remember that the dog food companies have prepared their food so that it is a balanced ration in itself, and, indeed, many dogs are raised on dog food alone. If you try to change this balance too much you are likely to upset your pet's digestion, and the dog will not be as well fed in the long run. Either kibble or meal is a good basic food, and the most economical way to feed your dog.

Milk is good for puppies and some grown dogs like it. Big bones are fine to chew on, especially for teething puppies, but small bones such as chicken, chop or fish bones are always dangerous; they may splinter or stick in the digestive tract. Table scraps such as meat, fat, or vegetables will furnish variety and vitamins, but fried or starchy foods such as potatoes and beans will not be of much food value. Adding a tablespoonful of fat (lard or drippings) to the daily food will keep your puppy's skin healthy and make his coat shine.

Remember that all dogs are individuals. It is the amount that will keep your dog in good health which is right for him, not the "rule-book" amount. A feeding chart to give you some idea of what the average puppy will eat follows:

A litter of Afghan puppies enjoying their meal in an outdoor pen.

WEANING TO 3 MONTHS: *A.M.* 1 cup dog food; mixed with warm water. *Noon* 1 cup milk; cereal, kibble, or biscuits. *P.M.* ½ cup dog food; ¼ lb. meat; 1 tbs. fat, scraps. *Bedtime* 1 cup milk; biscuit.

3—6 MONTHS: *A.M.* 2 cups dog meal or kibble, mixed. *Noon* 1 cup milk; soft-boiled egg twice a week. *P.M.* 1 cup meal, as above.

6 MONTHS—1 YEAR: *A.M.* 3 cups of dog meal; or milk with kibble. *P.M.* 2 cups of meal with ½ lb. meat, fat, scraps.

OVER 1 YEAR: *A.M.* half of evening meal if you prefer. *P.M.* 4-5 cups meal, as above.

Ch. Shirkhan of Grandeur proudly displays some of the trophies of his show career.

This Afghan is enjoying his meal; keep cool, fresh water available for your dog at all times. The snood around his neck is to protect his ears from getting messy.

To teach your dog to lie down, pull down on the leash from the sitting position, and at the same time say "Down."

You can try a system of self-feeding instead of giving your puppy regular meals. This means keeping the dry meal or kibble in front of him all the time. If he is inclined to overeat, put out only the daily amount each morning. Otherwise you can leave a filled dish or pail (protected from the weather and insects if outside) where he can nibble at leisure.

THE PUPPY'S BED

It is up to you to decide where the puppy will sleep. Unless it is winter in a cold climate, even a young puppy can sleep outside in a snug, well-built dog house. It should have a tight, pitched roof to let the rain run off, and a floor off the ground, to avoid dampness. The door should be no larger than the grown dog will need to go in and out, as a bigger opening lets in too much draft. For bedding you can use an old rag or blanket, straw, or sweet-smelling cedar shavings. Whether the puppy sleeps indoors or out, he will benefit from an outdoor run of his own where he can be put to exercise and amuse himself. It does not have to be large for if he goes for walks and plays with you he will get enough exercise that way. He is much safer shut in his run than being left loose to follow a stray dog off your property and get into bad habits—if he isn't hit by a car first!

Of course if the dog is left in his run for any length of time he should have protection from the cold, rain or sun. The run should be rectangular, and as big as you can conveniently make it up to 20 feet x 40 feet, with strong wire fence which will keep your dog in and intruders out. The wire should be at least four feet high, as many dogs like to jump, and the gate should be fastened with a spring hook or hasp which is not likely to be unfastened by mischance.

If your dog sleeps indoors, he should have his own place, and not be allowed to climb all over the furniture. He should sleep out of drafts, but not right next to the heat, which would make him too sensitive to the cold when he goes outside. If your youngster wants him to sleep on his bed, that is all right, too, but the puppy must learn the difference between his bed and other furniture. He may sleep on a dog bed or in a box big enough to curl up in: a regulation dog crate or one made from a packing box, with bedding for comfort. If your cellar is dry and fairly warm the puppy will be all right there, or in the garage.

You have already decided where the puppy will sleep before you bring him home. Let him stay there, or in the corner he will soon learn is "his," most of the time, so that he will gain a sense of security from the familiar. Give the puppy a little milk with bread or kibble in it when he arrives, but don't worry if he isn't hungry at first. He will soon develop an appetite when he grows accustomed to his surroundings. The first night the puppy may cry a bit from lonesomeness, but if he has an old blanket or rug to curl up in he will be cozy. In winter a hot water bottle will help replace the warmth of his littermates, or the ticking of a clock may provide company.

HOUSEBREAKING YOUR PUPPY

As soon as you get your puppy you can begin to housebreak him but remember that you can't expect too much of him until he is five months old or so. A baby puppy just cannot control himself, so it is best to give him an opportunity to relieve himself before the need arises.

Don't let the puppy wander through the whole house; keep him in one or two rooms under your watchful eye. If he sleeps in the house and has been brought up on newspapers, keep a couple of pages handy on the floor. When he starts to whimper, puts his nose to the ground or runs around looking restless, take him to the paper before an "accident" occurs. After he has behaved, praise him and let him roam again. It is much better to teach him the right way than to punish him for misbehaving. Puppies are

To housebreak your puppy keep paper in a corner of his room and take him there to relieve himself.

These puppies are the right age to become good friends with a youngster. Note that the puppy on the right has no mask.

Train your Afghan to sit by pulling up on the leash as you first press down on the hindquarters and say "Sit" in a firm tone of voice. Then give the command "Stay."

Mrs. Shay poses her famous Best in Show winner, Ch. Shirkhan, for the show ring.

naturally clean and can be housebroken easily, given the chance. If a mistake should occur, and mistakes are bound to happen, wash it immediately with tepid water, followed by another rinse with water to which a few drops of vinegar have been added. A dog will return to the same place if there is any odor left, so it is important to remove all traces.

If your puppy sleeps outside, housebreaking will be even easier. Remember that the puppy has to relieve himself after meals and whenever he wakes up, as well as sometimes in between. So take him outside as soon as he shows signs of restlessness indoors, and stay with him until he has performed. Then praise and pat him, and bring him back inside as a reward. Since he is used to taking care of himself outdoors, he will not want to misbehave in the house, and will soon let you know when he wants to go out.

You can combine indoor paper training and outdoor housebreaking by taking the puppy out when convenient and keeping newspaper available for use at other times. As the puppy grows older he will be able to control himself for longer periods. If he starts to misbehave in the house, without asking to go out first, scold him and take him out or to his paper. Punishment *after* the fact will accomplish nothing; the puppy cannot understand why he is being scolded unless it is immediate.

The older puppy or grown dog should be able to remain overnight in the house without needing to go out, unless he is ill. If your dog barks or acts restless, take him out once, but unless he relieves himself right away, take him back indoors and shut him in his quarters. No dog will soil his bed if he can avoid it, and your pet will learn to control himself overnight if he has to.

VETERINARY CARE

You will want your puppy to be protected against the most serious puppyhood diseases: distemper and infectious hepatitis. So your first action after getting him will be to take him to your veterinarian for his shots and a check-up, if he has not already received them. He may have had all or part of the immunization as early as two months, so check with the seller before you bring your puppy home.

You may give the puppy temporary serum which provides immunity for about two weeks, but nowadays permanent vaccine providing lifelong immunity can be given so early that the serum is seldom used, except as a precaution in outbreaks. The new vaccine is a combined one against distemper and hepatitis, and may be given in one or three (two weeks apart) shots. Your veterinarian probably has a preferred type, so go along with him, as either method is protective in a very high percentage of cases.

There is now an effective anti-rabies vaccine, which you can give to your dog if there should be an outbreak of this disease in your neighborhood. It is not permanent, however, so unless local regulations demand it, there is little value in giving the vaccine in ordinary circumstances.

Examine your dog's teeth regularly. This dog illustrates the perfect bite called for by Kennel Club Standards.

WORMING

Your puppy has probably been wormed at least once, since puppies have a way of picking up worms, particularly in a kennel where they are exposed to other dogs. Find out when he was last wormed and the date, if any, for re-worming. Older dogs are usually able to throw off worms if they are in good condition when infected, but unless the puppy is given

Mrs. Shay shows off a team of stunning Afghans.

This is the easy and correct way to groom your Afghan; have him stand on a platform and work upward on the coat.

After receiving the command to stay, your dog will wait until you call him or return to him.

Teach your Afghan to "heel" beside you on leash instead of tugging ahead or lagging.

some help when he gets worms, he is likely to become seriously sick. New worm medicines containing the non-toxic but effective piperazines may be bought at your pet store or druggist's, and you can give them yourself. But remember to follow instructions carefully and do not worm the puppy unless you are sure he has worms.

If the puppy passes a long, string-like white worm in his stool or coughs one up, that is sufficient evidence, and you should proceed to worm him. Other indications are: general listlessness, a large belly, dull coat, mattery eye and coughing, but these could also be signs that your puppy is coming down with some disease. If you only *suspect* that he has worms, take him to your veterinarian for a check-up and stool examination before worming.

THE FEMALE PUPPY

If you want to spay your female you can have it done while she is still a puppy. Her first seasonal period may occur as early as nine months, although the average Afghan female starts at about 16 months. She may be spayed before or after this, or you may breed her and still spay her afterward.

The first sign of the female's being in season is a thin red discharge, which will increase for about a week, when it changes color to a thin yellowish stain, lasting about another week. Simultaneously there is a swelling of the vulva, the dog's external sexual organ. The second week is the crucial period, when she could be bred if you wanted her to have puppies, but it is possible for the period to be shorter or longer, so it is best not to take unnecessary risks at any time. After a third week the swelling decreases and the period is over for about six months.

The female will probably lose her puppy coat, or at least shed out part of it, about three months after she is in season, for this is the time when her puppies would be weaned, if she had been mated, and females generally drop coat at that time.

If you have an absolutely climb-proof and dig-proof run, within your yard, it will be safe to leave her there, but otherwise the female in season should be shut indoors. Don't leave her out alone for even a minute; she should be exercised only on leash. If you want to prevent the neighborhood dogs from hanging around your doorstep, as they inevitably will as soon as they discover that your female is in season, take her some distance away from the house before you let her relieve herself. Take her to a nearby park or field in the car for a chance to stretch her legs. After the three weeks are up you can let her out as before, with no worry that she can have puppies until the next season. But if you want to have her spayed, consult your veterinarian about the time and age at which he prefers to do it. With a young dog the operation is simple and after a night or two at the animal hospital she can be at home, wearing only a small bandage as a souvenir.

4. Caring for Your Adult Afghan

When your dog reaches his first birthday he is no longer a puppy, although he will not be fully mature and developed until he is two. For all intents and purposes, however, he may be considered full-grown and adult, now.

DIET

You may prefer to continue feeding your dog twice a day, although he can now eat all that he needs to be healthy at one meal a day. Usually it is best to feed that one meal, or the main meal, in the evening. Most dogs eat better this way, and digest their food better. If your dog skips an occasional meal, don't worry; after half an hour remove the food if he turns up his nose at it. Otherwise he will develop the habit of picking at his food, and food left out too long becomes stale or spoiled. If you use the dry self-feeding method, of course this does not apply.

The best indication of the correct amount to feed your dog is his state of health. A fat dog is not a healthy one; just like a fat person, he has to strain his heart—and his whole body—to carry excess weight. If you cannot give your dog more exercise, cut down on his food, and remember that those dog biscuits fed as snacks or rewards count in the calories. If your dog is thin, increase the amount and add a little more fat. You can also add flavoring he likes to pep up his appetite. The average grown dog needs 5 to 6 cups of dog meal, or a pound of canned food with an additional two cups of meal, per day. Use your own judgment for YOUR dog.

But remember that the Afghan is normally thin; while another breed would be out of condition, it is proper for the Afghan to show his prominent hip bones and spine.

CLEANLINESS AND GROOMING

In spite of his luxuriant coat, the Afghan needs little in the way of grooming. If you want to keep his coat thick and long, by all means spare the comb, which will pull out the hairs. The more coat care you give, the more beautiful your Afghan will become, but as his owner you need not be

A trio of magnificent Afghans: a black, a fawn and a blue.
Note topknots and beards.

a slave to the grooming brush. For practical purposes a weekly brushing, properly done, will keep him in good condition.

You should establish good grooming habits while your dog is a young puppy. Even though his coat is short and does not need brushing, the puppy should learn to stand for the operation, preferably on a bench or table. When he is full grown, brushing will be easier if the dog stands quietly at a convenient height. Equipment should include a bristle brush (which will not tear the coat) and a steel comb. Brush from the skin out, starting with the lower legs and body; hold the hair with the left hand and brush downward with the right. Move upward, gradually allowing the hair to fall and be brushed. Cover the entire body this way. Don't neglect the underparts or behind the ears, but take care not to pull out the coat.

If you meet knots or snarls, pull them apart with your fingers and then tease them out with the comb. Really bad knots should be saturated with a grooming oil and then worked out. As a last resort, use scissors to cut the knot and then work the hairs apart. This care will assure a smooth, "finished looking" coat. The correct texture is not woolly, but silky, fitting the line of the body, never bushy. A puppy's coat develops gradually, full length coming at about four years. The coat should never be oiled, but can be bathed as often as necessary.

The Afghan will seldom need a bath unless he gets into something smelly or is so dirty it won't brush out. For a bath, use one of the special dog soaps, a shampoo made for humans, or soap pieces dissolved to make a solution. Be sure to rinse all the soap out so that no residue will be left to irritate the skin. Adding a few drops of vinegar to the last rinse is good for the skin. Use towels to dry your Afghan afterward. If the weather is cool keep him in a warm place to prevent chilling. Too much bathing will dry the skin and cause shedding, so don't overdo it in any event. Few long-haired dogs have much natural enthusiasm for water, but if your Afghan likes to swim, he will get enough bathing that way.

If your dog's skin is dry or he sheds more than a few hairs when groomed, it may be due to lack of fat in his diet. Add more bacon fat or lard to his food, making it two-three instead of one tbs. Other skin troubles, shown by scratching, redness, or a sore on the surface, should be examined by your veterinarian, who can prescribe treatment and clear up the trouble quickly. Don't delay, as once it takes hold any skin disease is hard to cure, particularly with a long-haired dog.

NOSE, TEETH, EARS AND EYES

Normally a dog's nose, teeth, ears and eyes need no special care. The dog's nose is cool and moist to the touch (unless he has been in a warm house); however, the "cold nose" theory is only a partial indication of health or sickness. A fever, for instance, would be shown by a hot, dry nose, but

Be careful not to get soap in his eyes or leave any in his coat when bathing your Afghan. A spray nozzle is fine for rinsing.

Be sure after bathing to dry your Afghan thoroughly to prevent chills.

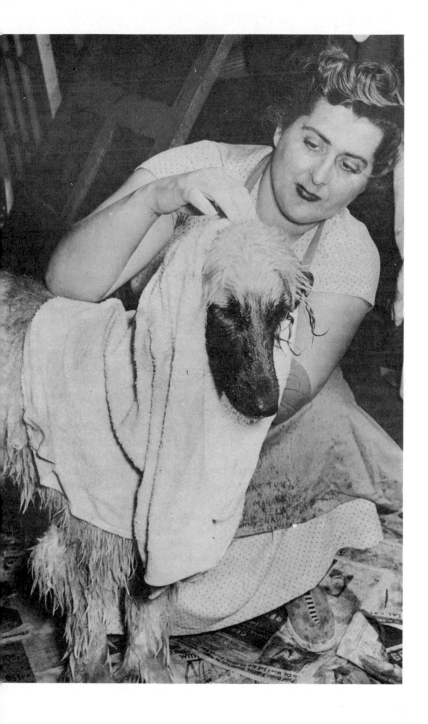

other illness might not cause this. The dog's eyes are normally bright and alert, with the eyelid down in the corner, not over the eye. If the haw is bloodshot or partially covers the eye, it may be a sign of illness, or irritation. If your dog has matter in the corners of the eyes, bathe with a mild eye wash; obtain ointment from your veterinarian or pet shop to treat a chronic condition.

If your dog seems to have something wrong with his ears which causes him to scratch at them or shake his head, cautiously probe the ear with a cotton swab. An accumulation of wax will probably work itself out. But dirt or dried blood is indicative of ear mites or infection, and should be treated immediately. Sore ears in the summer, due to fly bites, should be washed with mild soap and water, then covered with a soothing ointment, gauze-wrapped if necessary. Keep the dog protected from insects, inside if necessary, until his ears heal.

The dog's teeth will take care of themselves, although you may want your veterinarian to scrape off the unsightly tartar accumulation occasionally. A good hard bone will help to do the same thing.

PARASITES

Should your dog pick up fleas or other skin parasites from neighbors' dogs or from the ground, weekly use of a good DDT- or Chlordane-base flea powder will keep them off. Remember to dust his bed and change the bedding, too, as flea eggs drop off the host to hatch and wait in likely places for the dog to return. In warm weather a weekly dusting or monthly dip is good prevention.

If your grown dog is well fed and in good health you will probably have no trouble with worms. He may pick them up from other dogs, however, so if you suspect worms, have a stool examination made and, if necessary, worm him. Fleas, too, are carriers of tapeworm, so that is one good reason to make sure the dog is free from these insects. Roundworms, the dog's most common intestinal parasite, have a life cycle which permits complete eradication by worming twice, ten days apart. The first worming will remove all adults and the second will destroy all subsequently hatched eggs before they in turn can produce more parasites.

FIRST AID

Should your dog be injured, you can give him first aid which is, in general, similar to that for a human. The same principles apply. Superficial wounds should be disinfected and healing ointment applied. If the cut is likely to get dirty apply a bandage and restrain the dog so that he won't keep trying to remove it. A cardboard ruff will prevent him from licking his chest or body. Nails can be taped down to prevent scratching.

Here is the proper way to cut your Afghan's nails with clippers: push the hair back so you can see, and don't cut too much.

A board splint should be put on before moving a dog which might have a broken bone. If you are afraid that the dog will bite from pain, use a bandage muzzle made from a long strip of cloth, wrapped around the muzzle, then tied under the jaw and brought up behind the ears to hold it on. In case of severe bleeding apply a tourniquet—a strip of cloth wrapped around a stick to tighten it will do—between the cut on a limb and the heart, but loosen it every few minutes to avoid damaging the circulation.

If you suspect that your dog has swallowed poison, try to get him to vomit by giving him salt water or mustard in water. In all these cases, rush him to your veterinarian as soon as possible, after alerting him by phone.

In warm weather the most important thing to remember for your dog's sake is providing fresh water. If he tends to slobber and drink too much,

The proper way to give a pill: put it in the back of the dog's throat and hold his mouth closed until he swallows.

it may be offered at intervals of an hour or so instead of being available at all times, but it should be fresh and cool. Don't over-exercise the dog or let the children play too wildly with him in the heat of the day. Don't leave him outside without shade, and never leave a dog in a car which could become overheated in the sun. It should always have some shade and ventilation through the windows.

A long-coated breed like the Afghan has built-in air-conditioning, so NEVER clip him, but have his welfare constantly in mind during warm weather.

THE OLD DOG

With the increased knowledge and care available, there is no reason why your dog should not live to a good old age. As he grows older he may need a little additional care, however. Remember that a fat dog is not healthy, particularly as he grows older, and limit his food accordingly. The older dog needs exercise as much as ever, although his heart cannot bear the strain of sudden and violent exertion. His digestion may not be as good as it was as a puppy, so follow your veterinarian's advice about special feeding, if necessary. Failing eyesight or hearing mean lessened awareness of dangers, so you must protect him more than before. The old dog is used to his home, and to set ways, so too many strangers are bound to be a strain. For the same reason, boarding him out or a trip to the vet's are to be avoided unless absolutely necessary.

Should you decide at this time to get a puppy, to avoid being without a dog when your old retainer is no longer with you, be very careful how you introduce the puppy. He is naturally playful and will expect the older dog to respond to his advances. Sometimes the old dog will get a new lease on life from a pup. But don't make him jealous by giving to the newcomer the attention that formerly was exclusively his. Feed them apart, and show the old dog that you still love him the most; the puppy, not being used to individual attention will not mind sharing your love.

5. Caring for the Female and Raising Puppies

Whether or not you bought your female dog intending to breed her, some preparation is necessary when and if you decide to take this step.

WHEN TO BREED

It is usually best to breed on the second or third season. Plan in advance the time of year which is best for you, taking into account where the puppies will be born and raised. You will keep them until they are at least six weeks old, and a litter of husky pups takes up considerable space by then. Other considerations are selling the puppies (Christmas vs. springtime sales), your own vacation, and time available to care for them. You'll need at least an hour a day to feed and clean up after the mother and puppies but probably it will take you much longer—with time out to admire and play with them!

CHOOSING THE STUD

You can plan to breed your female about 6½ months after the start of her last season, although a variation of a month or two either way is not unusual. Choose the stud dog and make arrangements well in advance. If you are breeding for show stock, which may command better prices, a mate should be chosen with an eye to complementing the deficiencies of your female. If possible, they should have several ancestors in common within the last two or three generations, as such combinations generally "click" best. He should have a good show record or be the sire of show winners if old enough to be proven.

The owner of such a male usually charges a fee for the use of the dog of $150 or more. This does not guarantee a litter, but you generally have the right to breed your female again if she does not have puppies. In some cases the owner of the stud will agree to take a choice puppy in place of a stud fee. You should settle all details beforehand, including the possibility of a single surviving puppy, deciding the age at which he is to make his choice and take the pup, and so on.

If you want to raise a litter "just for the fun of it" and plan merely to make use of an available male, the most important selection point is temperament. Make sure the dog is friendly as well as healthy, because a bad disposition could appear in his puppies, and this is the worst of all traits in a dog destined to be a pet. In such cases a "stud fee puppy," not necessarily the choice of the litter, is the usual payment.

PREPARATION FOR BREEDING

Before you breed your female, make sure she is in good health. She should be neither too thin nor too fat. Any skin disease *must* be cured, before it can be passed on to the puppies. If she has worms she should be wormed before being bred or within three weeks afterward. It is generally considered a good idea to revaccinate her against distemper and hepatitis before the puppies are born. This will increase the immunity the puppies receive during their early, most vulnerable period.

The female will probably be ready to breed 12 days after the first colored discharge. You can usually make arrangements to board her with the owner of the male for a few days, to insure her being there at the proper time, or you can take her to be mated and bring her home the same day. If she still appears receptive she may be bred again two days later. However, some females never show signs of willingness, so it helps to have the experience of a breeder. Usually the second day after the discharge changes color is the proper time, and she may be bred for about three days following. For an additional week or so she may have some discharge and attract other dogs by her odor, but can seldom be bred.

THE FEMALE IN WHELP

You can expect the puppies nine weeks from the day of breeding, although 61 days is as common as 63. During this time the female should receive normal care and exercise. If she was overweight, don't increase her food at first; excess weight at whelping time is bad. If she is on the thin side build her up, giving some milk and biscuit at noon if she likes it. You may add one of the mineral and vitamin supplements to her food, to make sure that the puppies will be healthy. As her appetite increases, feed her more. During the last two weeks the puppies grow enormously and she will probably have little room for food and less appetite. She should be tempted with meat, liver and milk, however.

As the female in whelp grows heavier, cut out violent exercise and jumping. Although a dog used to such activities will often play with the children or run around voluntarily, restrain her for her own sake.

An approaching sign of whelping is loss of hair around the breasts.

This should be combed out, or cut if she does not shed, as it will be in the puppies' way, and the long skirts too, as they will be dirty.

PREPARING FOR THE PUPPIES

Prepare a whelping box a few days before the puppies are due, and allow the mother to sleep there overnight or to spend some time in it during the day to become accustomed to it. Then she is less likely to try to have her pups under the front porch or in the middle of your bed. A variety of places will serve such as a corner of your cellar, garage, or an unused room. If the weather is warm, a large outdoor doghouse will do, well protected from rain or draft. A whelping box serves to separate mother and puppies from visitors and other distractions. The walls should be high enough to restrain the puppies, yet allow the mother to get away from the puppies after she has fed them. Four feet square is minimum size, and one-foot walls will keep the pups in until they begin to climb, when it should be built up. Then the puppies really need more room anyway, so double the space with a very low partition down the middle and you will find them naturally housebreaking themselves.

Layers of newspaper spread over the whole area will make excellent bedding and be absorbent enough to keep the surface warm and dry. They should be removed daily and replaced with another thick layer. An old quilt or washable blanket makes better footing for the nursing puppies than slippery newspaper during the first week, and is softer for the mother.

Be prepared for the actual whelping several days in advance. Usually the female will tear up papers, refuse food and generally act restless. These may be false alarms; the real test is her temperature, which will drop to below 100° about 12 hours before whelping. Take it with a rectal thermometer morning and evening, and put her in the pen, looking in on her frequently, when the temperature goes down.

WHELPING

Usually little help is needed but it is wise to stay close to make sure that the mother's lack of experience does not cause an unnecessary accident. Be ready to help when the first puppy arrives, for it could smother if she does not break the membrane enclosing it. She should start right away to lick the puppy, drying and stimulating it, but you can do it with a soft rough towel, instead. The afterbirth should follow the birth of each puppy, attached to the puppy by the long umbilical cord. Watch to make sure that each is expelled, anyway, for retaining this material can cause infection. In her instinct for cleanliness the mother will probably eat the afterbirth after biting the cord. One or two will not hurt her; they stimulate milk supply as well as labor for remaining pups. But too many can make her lose appetite for the food she needs to feed her pups and regain her strength.

A dog bed like this in a quiet corner is a fine place for an Afghan to sleep.

So remove the rest of them along with the wet newspapers and keep the pen dry and clean to relieve her anxiety.

If the mother does not bite the cord, or does it too close to the body, take over the job, to prevent an umbilical hernia. Tearing is recommended, but you can cut it, about two inches from the body, with a sawing motion of scissors, sterilized in alcohol. Then dip the end in a shallow dish of iodine; the cord will dry up and fall off in a few days.

The puppies should follow each other at intervals of not more than half an hour. If more time goes past and you are sure there are still pups to come, a brisk walk outside may start labor again. If she is actively straining without producing a puppy it may be presented backward, a so-called "breach" or upside down birth. Careful assistance with a well-soaped finger to feel for the puppy or ease it back may help, but never attempt to pull it by force against the mother. This could cause serious damage, so let an expert handle it.

If anything seems wrong, waste no time in calling your veterinarian who can examine her and if necessary give hormones which will bring the remaining puppies. You may want his experience in whelping the litter even if all goes well. He will probably prefer to have the puppies born at his hospital rather than to get up in the middle of the night to come to your home. The mother would, no doubt, prefer to stay at home, but you can be sure she will get the best of care in his hospital. If the puppies are born at home and all goes as it should, watch the mother carefully afterward.

It is wise to have the veterinarian check her and the pups.

RAISING THE PUPPIES

Hold each puppy to a breast as soon as he is dry, for a good meal without competition. Then he may join his littermates in the basket, out of his mother's way while she is whelping. Keep a supply of evaporated milk on hand for emergencies, or later weaning. A formula of evaporated milk, corn syrup and a little water with egg yolk should be warmed and fed in a doll or baby bottle if necessary. A supplementary feeding often helps weak pups over the hump. Keep track of birth weights, and weekly readings, thereafter; it will furnish an accurate record of the pups' growth and health.

After the puppies have arrived, take the mother outside for a walk and drink, and then leave her to take care of them. She will probably not want to stay away more than a minute or two for the first few weeks. Be sure to keep water available at all times, and feed her milk or broth frequently, as she needs liquids to produce milk. Encourage her to eat, with her favorite foods, until she asks for it of her own accord. She will soon develop a ravenous appetite and should have at least two large meals a day, with dry food available in addition.

Prepare a warm place to put the puppies after they are born to keep them dry and help them to a good start in life. An electric heating pad or hot water bottle covered with flannel in the bottom of a cardboard box should be set near the mother so that she can see her puppies. She will usually allow you to help, but don't take the puppies out of sight, and let her handle things if your interference seems to make her nervous.

Be sure that all the puppies are getting enough to eat. If the mother, sits or stands, instead of lying still to nurse, the probable cause is scratching from the puppies' nails. You can remedy this by clipping them, as you do hers. Manicure scissors will do for these tiny claws. Some breeders advise disposing of the smaller or weaker pups in a large litter, as the mother has trouble in handling more than six or seven. But you can help her out by preparing an extra puppy box or basket. Leave half the litter with the mother and the other half in a warm place, changing off at two hour intervals at first. Later you may change them less frequently, leaving them all together except during the day. Try supplementary feeding, too; as soon as their eyes open, at about two weeks, they will lap from a dish, anyway.

WEANING THE PUPPIES

The puppies should normally be completely weaned at five weeks, although you start to feed them at three weeks. They will find it easier to lap semi-solid food than to drink milk at first, so mix baby cereal with whole or evaporated milk, warmed to body temperature, and offer it to the puppies in a saucer. Until they learn to lap it is best to feed one or two at a time, because they are more likely to walk into it than to eat. Hold the saucer at chin level, and let them gather around, keeping paws out of the dish. A damp sponge afterward prevents most of the cereal from sticking to the skin if the mother doesn't clean them up. Once they have gotten the idea, broth or babies' meat soup may be alternated with milk, and you can start them on finely chopped meat. At four weeks they will eat four meals a day, and soon do without their mother entirely. Start them on mixed dog food, or leave it with them in a dish for self-feeding. Don't leave water with them all the time; at this age everything is to play with and they will use it as a wading pool. They can drink all they need if it is offered several times a day, after meals.

As the puppies grow up the mother will go into the pen only to nurse them, first sitting up and then standing. To dry her up completely, keep the mother away for longer periods; after a few days of part-time nursing she can stay away for longer periods, and then completely. The little milk left will be resorbed.

The puppies may be put outside, unless it is too cold, as soon as their eyes are open, and will benefit from the sunlight and vitamins. A rubber mat or newspapers underneath will protect them from cold or damp. At six weeks they can go outside permanently unless it is very cold, but make sure that they go into their shelter at night or in bad weather. By now cleaning up is a man-sized job, so put them out at least during the day and make your task easier. Be sure to clean their run daily, as worms and other infections are lurking. You can expect the pups to need at least one worming before they are ready to go to new homes, so take a stool sample to your veterinarian before they are three weeks old. If one puppy has worms all should be wormed. Follow the veterinarian's advice, and this applies also to vaccination. If you plan to keep a pup you will want to vaccinate him at the earliest age, so his littermates should be done at the same time.

6. How to Train Your Afghan

ANIMAL OR PET?

There is only a one-word difference between an *animal* and a *pet* and that word is TRAINING.

But training your dog depends upon many factors:

how intelligent you are;

how intelligent the dog is;

what your intentions are;

how much time you are willing to devote to the task.

First we consider the dog owner who is merely interested in training his dog to be a perfect home companion, a dog that he can be proud to own, a dog that won't embarrass him by untimely "accidents" nor kill himself by running into the street.

THE DOG OWNER'S PART

Before you begin training your dog to be a pet, there are certain important facts to remember:

You are a human being and do not speak the same language that a dog does. So you must try to think as a pet dog thinks; your dog will try to understand his trainer.

Training your dog is like training a child. It requires firmness tempered with kindness, strictness but gentleness, consistency, repetition and above all PATIENCE. You must have the patience to go over the training cycle time and time again until the message reaches your dog.

Did you know that a dog is the only known animal that can be bribed into learning by just a few kind words and soft pats on the back? Other animals must be bribed with food or be beaten into submission, but not your pet dog. He wants kindness and attention. Reward him with a pat on the back when he is doing well and you will soon have a dog eager to learn.

You can easily train your dog to become a well-behaved member of your family. Training should begin the day you get him. Although a puppy under six months is too young to expect much in the way of obedience, you should teach him to respect your authority. Be consistent. Don't allow the pup to jump all over you when you are wearing old clothes, because you can't expect him to know the difference when you are dressed for a party. Don't encourage the dog to climb into your lap or onto your bed, then punish him for leaving hair on furniture when you aren't around. Although six months to a year is the best time to begin serious training, a dog of any age can learn if taught with consideration and patience. You *can* teach an old dog new tricks.

Housebreaking has already been covered. You cannot expect perfection from a puppy, or even an older dog, particularly if he is not used to living in a house. Going into a strange place, a dog is likely to be ill at ease and make a mistake for that reason. Remember that once it has happened, the only way to prevent further accidents is to avoid the opportunity and to be sure to remove traces which would remind the dog of previous errors.

After you have taught your dog to be clean indoors and to relieve himself outside, you should teach him to do it on command, not only in one familiar place. It is a convenience when traveling to be able to keep him on leash, so take the time to teach him before it is necessary. "Curb your dog" is the rule in most cities; for the sake of others you should teach your dog to obey it.

GIVING COMMANDS

When you give commands use the shortest phrase possible and use the same word with the same meaning at all times. If you want to teach your dog to sit, then always use the word SIT. If you want your dog to lie down, then always use the word DOWN. It doesn't matter what word you use as long as your dog becomes accustomed to hearing it and acts upon it.

The trick hound dog that always sits on the command UP and stands on the command SIT was easily trained to understand the words that way. The words are merely sounds to him. He cannot understand you but he understands the tone of your voice and the inflection of the words.

Unless you are consistent in your use of commands you can never train your animal properly.

WHAT ABOUT LESSONS?

Try to make your training lessons interesting and appealing both to yourself and your dog. Short frequent lessons are of much more value than long lessons. It is much better for all concerned if you teach your dog for 10 minutes at a time, three times a day, than for 30 minutes once a day. The 10 minute session amuses both you and your dog and the attachment which develops between you during these lessons will be everlasting.

A good time to train your dog is for 10 minutes before you give him his breakfast; then he assumes that the meal is a reward for his being such a good dog. If you follow this schedule for all three meals your training program will be extremely successful.

WHAT YOU WILL TEACH YOUR DOG

Your house pet should certainly learn the rudiments necessary to good behavior. Your dog should be housebroken first of all. Then he should learn how to walk properly with a collar and leash, after which he should be taught the simple commands of HEEL, SIT, COME and STAY. Only after the dog has learned these commands is it safe to train him off the leash.

Once your dog gets into the swing of his training it is wise to continue to train him in more difficult performances. After all, the hardest part of the job is establishing a communication system so that each of you learns what to expect from the other. Once your dog learns a trick or a command he will hardly ever forget it if you repeat it every so often. Begging, giving his paw, playing dead and rolling over, are entertaining tricks which you, your friends and your dog can all enjoy to mutual benefit. There are, however, more important lessons first.

COLLAR AND LEASH

Your puppy should become used to a leash and collar at an early age. He seldom needs a license until he is six months old, and a leather collar will be outgrown several times before then. Buy one for use, not looks or permanence. A thin chain "choke collar" is a good substitute, but you will want a larger and slightly heavier one for training later on. Never leave a choke on a loose dog, for it could catch on something and strangle him. If you want to use one as a permanent collar, buy a clip to fasten the two ends, so that it cannot choke him.

Let the puppy wear his collar around until he is used to its feel and weight. After several short periods he will not be distracted by the strangeness and you can attach the leash. Let him pull it around and then try to lead him a bit. He will probably resist, bucking and balking, or simply sit down and refuse to budge. Fight him for a few minutes, dragging him along if necessary, but then let him relax for the day, with plenty of affection and praise. He won't be lead-broken until he learns that he must obey the pull under any circumstance, but don't try to do it in one lesson. Ten minutes a day is long enough for any training. The dog's period of concentration is short and, like a child, he will become bored if you carry it on too long.

This young Afghan and his owner are ready to start training lessons on collar and leash.

This Afghan is wearing a leather slip-collar show lead, which is also satisfactory for out walking.

TRAINING YOUR DOG TO WALK PROPERLY

After your dog has been housebroken and has become accustomed to his collar or harness you must teach him to walk properly on a leash. We are assuming that you will use the collar and leash when housebreaking your puppy. Once he is thoroughly familiar with the workings of these restraining objects, you must teach him to respect the master at the other end of the leash.

You should hold the leash firmly in your right hand. The dog should walk on your left side with the leash crossing the front of your body. The reason for this will be obvious once you've actually walked your dog . . . you have more control this way.

Let your dog lead you for the first few moments so that he fully understands that freedom can be his if he goes about it properly. He knows already that when he wants to go outdoors the leash and collar are necessary, so he has respect for the leash. Now, if while walking, he starts to pull in one direction all you do is *stop walking*. He will walk a few steps and then find that he can't walk any further. He will then turn and look into your face. *This is the crucial point.* Just stand there for a moment and stare right back at him . . . Now walk another ten feet and stop again. Again your dog will probably walk out the leash, find he can't go any further, and turn around and look again. If he starts to pull and jerk then just stand there. After he quiets down, just bend down and comfort him as he may be frightened. Keep up this training until he learns not to outwalk you.

Once the puppy obeys the pull of the leash half your training is accomplished. "Heeling" is a necessity for a well-behaved dog, so teach him to walk beside you, head even with your knee. Nothing looks sadder than a big dog taking his helpless owner for a walk. It is annoying to passers-by and other dog owners to have a large dog, however friendly, bear down on them and entangle dogs, people and packages.

To teach your dog, start off walking briskly, saying "Heel" in a firm voice. Pull back with a sharp jerk if he lunges ahead, and if he lags repeat the command and tug on the leash, not allowing him to drag behind. After the dog has learned to heel at various speeds on leash, you can remove it and practice heeling free, but have it ready to snap on again as soon as he wanders.

You must understand that most dogs like to stop and sniff around a bit until they find THE place to do their duty. Be kind enough to stop and wait when they find it necessary to pause. This is the whole story . . . it's as easy as that. A smart dog can learn to walk properly in a few days, provided you have taught him correctly from the beginning. A dog that is incorrectly trained initially may take a month to retrain, but in any event, every dog can learn to walk properly on a leash!

TEACHING YOUR DOG TO COME, SIT AND STAY

When the dog understands the pull of the leash he should learn to come. Never call him to you for punishment, or he will be quick to disobey. (Always go to him if he has been disobedient.) To teach him to come, let him reach the end of a long lead, then give the command, pulling him toward you at the same time. As soon as he associates the word "Come" with the action, pull only when he does not respond immediately. As he starts to come, back up to make him learn that he must come from a distance as well as when he is close to you. Soon you can practice without a leash, but if he is slow to come or actively disobedient, go to him and pull him toward you, repeating the command. More practice with leash on is needed.

Your dog has been named and he knows his name. After hearing his name called over and over again in your home, he finds that it pays to come when called. Why? Because you only call him when his food is ready or when you wish to play with him and pet him. Outside the house it is a different story. He would rather play by himself or with other dogs or chase a cat than play with you. So, he must be trained to come to you when he is called.

"Sit," "Down," and "Stay" are among the most useful commands and will make it easier for you to control your dog on many occasions—when grooming him, when he needs veterinary care, out walking if you meet a strange dog, or in the car, to mention a few. Teaching him to sit is the first step. With collar and leash on have him stand in the "Heel" position. Give the command, "Sit," at the same time pulling up on the leash in your right hand and pressing down on his hindquarters with your left. As soon as he sits, release the pressure and praise him.

To teach your dog to stay, bring your hand close to his face with a direct motion, at the same time as you give the order. Ask him to remain only a few seconds at first, but gradually the time can be increased and you can leave him at a distance. If he should move, return immediately and make him sit and stay again, after scolding him.

TRAINING YOUR DOG TO STOP WITHOUT COMMAND

When your dog has been trained to HEEL on a loose leash, the next step in his training is to STOP without command so that if you stop for a street corner or to talk to someone along the way, your dog doesn't pull you to get going. Training to stop without command requires use of the choke chain collar for the first lessons.

Take your dog out for his usual walk, keeping him at HEEL all the time. Then stop dead in your tracks keeping the leash tight in your hands without a bit of slack. DO NOT LET HIM SIT DOWN! No command is necessary. As soon as he stops, pat him on the back and give him some dog candy. Then

Train your dog to stand by placing his feet correctly and saying "Stay." Praise him when he obeys.

walk on again briskly and stop short. Keep your dog on the tight leash at all times and repeat this until he learns that he must stop dead in his tracks just as you do. When you stop, stop *deliberately* so that he can actually anticipate your stopping and be with you at all times. You can tell when he is being attentive for he will walk a few steps and then turn his head so that he can keep an eye on your face. He will actually crave to satisfy you once he has been properly taught, and he will only take a few steps before he swings his head to look at you. Next time you see a well-trained dog walking along the street, notice how much time he spends looking at his master instead of at other things.

Once your dog has learned to stop without command and you want to walk again, you can signal him by many means. One way is to slacken your leash and then start walking so that he will learn that a slackened leash means you intend to walk again. Another way is to signal him verbally with the word "Go" or "Come on Pal" or something similar to that. It doesn't matter what word you use as long as you use the same word all the time.

OFF-THE-LEASH TRAINING

After your dog has accomplished these lessons it is time to begin his training without a leash. Try to find a large open area which is fenced in. It will be safer to advance to this stage within the confines of that area. If no such area is available, find as quiet a street as you can (even late at night so that few automobiles are around) and begin your training there.

Let's assume that your dog heels and stops without command. After you've walked him a few feet and tested him on stopping without command, bend down and remove the leash. Start walking briskly as you did when training him to heel. Stop suddenly without command and see if he does the same. If he doesn't, then immediately snap on the leash with the choke collar and go through the training again. Walk once with the leash on and once with the leash off, until finally your dog gets the idea that he can have more freedom by behaving himself, than misbehaving. Don't forget to carry some dog candy along with you so you can reward him for a successful performance.

It is important for you and your dog to use his regular collar during "off-training" hours, since your dog likes a recess every few days. Then when you put on the training collar he knows that something new is coming along. Every time you put on the training collar give him a piece of candy and an extra pat or two. Let him know that both of you are going to enjoy the new experience.

TRAINING YOUR DOG TO LIE DOWN

To teach your dog to lie down, have him sit facing you. Pull down on the leash by putting your foot on it and pulling at the same time as you say "Down." Gesture toward the ground with a sweep of your arm. When he begins to understand what is wanted, do it without the leash and alternate voice and hand signals. Teach him to lie down from standing as well as sitting position, and begin to do it from a distance. Hand signals are particularly useful when your dog can see you but is too far away to hear, and they may be used in teaching all commands.

When giving the hand signal be careful that your dog doesn't think you are threatening him. You can dispel this fear by immediately offering him some dog candy each time he successfully completes the lying down maneuver.

To teach your Afghan to lie down, use the leverage of your foot to pull down, and simultaneously use hand signal and voice command.

DISCIPLINE TRAINING FOR YOUR DOG

Up to this point you have been training your dog to act upon command. Now you will attempt to train his intelligence. This is another important part of the training problem and it is the part that separates a "smart" dog from one that doesn't "use his head."

All dogs, regardless of their training, will get the urge to run after another dog, to chase a cat, to fetch, or just to run for the sheer love of running. In the open field or park this is perfectly all right, but in the city it can be catastrophic! Let's assume that your dog has a bad habit of slipping off his collar and making a mad dash away from you. You may find this out some fine, bright morning when both of you are in fine spirits: He will spot a cat, and without warning will dash off, either pulling the leash right out of your unwary hands or slipping his head out of the collar. A moment of panic will hit you both. But, once the initial impact of the moment is over, he will come scampering back at the command COME.

At this point do not beat your dog. He knows he has done something wrong and he is a bit confused himself. Just pat him on the head and ignore it . . . *this time*. Then walk back to the house and get a long rope, 25 to 30 feet long. Tie this rope to his regular collar (do not use a choke chain) and also use the regular leash. Try to get your dog into the same situation as the one he bolted from. When he runs away from you again (if he does), drop the leash but hold onto the rope. When he gets far enough away give a loud holler STOP and jerk the rope at the same time. He will spin in his tracks and lay where he is, thoroughly confused and a bit scared.

Go over to him and make a big fuss over him as though you can't imagine what happened. Tell him he should never have left your side. Repeat this training four or five times and he will never bolt from you again.

You can practice the command STOP by running a few steps with him and then shouting the command STOP as you suddenly stop short. By repeating the command STOP in every such situation it won't be too long before you can make your dog STOP on a dime!

TRAINING YOUR DOG NOT TO JUMP ON PEOPLE

Some dogs are so affectionate that they will jump on everybody who comes into sight in order to get their attention and affection. Only you can train your dog not to jump and it's an easy trick to learn. As he jumps up to greet *you,* merely bend your knee so he hits it with his chest and falls over. He cannot see your knee coming up as his head will be above your knee. After a few falls he will get the idea that it isn't practical to jump up to greet you or anyone.

Of course if he has learned the meaning of the command DOWN, then use that command when he jumps up. He won't like to assume the down position when he is anxious for a pat or piece of dog candy, so this will be an easy lesson for him to learn.

Standing erect, the Afghan shows his impressive size. If you don't want him to jump on you, say "No" as you push him down; he'll learn quickly.

Be firm with your dog if you do not want him on the furniture.

KEEPING YOUR DOG OFF THE FURNITURE

Your favorite sofa or chair will also be your dog's favorite seat. It is naturally used the most and so will have the odors (which only your dog can smell) of the beloved master. There are two ways of training your dog out of the habit of sitting in your chair. (You will want to break the habit because most dogs shed and their hair gets all over your clothes. Then again, he might like to curl up in your lap while you are trying to read or knit.)

The simplest way of breaking the habit is to soak a small rag with a special dog scent which is repulsive to dogs. Put the rag on the chair which your dog favors. He will jump on the chair, get a whiff of the scent and make a detour of the chair forever more!

Another way to train is to pull him off the chair every time you catch him there and immediately command him to lie DOWN at your feet. Then give him a severe tongue lashing. After a few times he will never go to the chair again WHILE YOU ARE AROUND! The greater problem is to teach him to stay away all the time. The usual plan is to get a few inexpensive mouse traps and set them (without bait of course) with a few sheets of newspaper over them. As soon as your dog jumps onto the chair the mouse-trap goes SNAP and off the chair goes the dog. He may try it again, but then the second trap will go off, and he will have learned his lesson.

Since your dog has his own bed, train him to stay in it when you don't want him to be any place else. This can be done by saying the word BED in a loud voice and dragging him over and placing him in it. Do this a few times and he will learn where to go when you want him in bed!

TRAINING YOUR DOG TO DO TRICKS

Nearly every housedog learns a few tricks without training during the course of his puppyhood. These are usually accidentally learned, but the master observes the dog doing them and then prompts him to repeat the same thing over and over again.

You will deliberately want to train your dog to shake hands. First get him into the sitting position. Then upon the command PAW, lift his paw in your hand and shake it vigorously without knocking him off balance. Then give him a piece of dog candy. Repeat this several times a day and in a week he will all but hold out his paw when you walk in the door!

Teaching your dog to beg is done in the same manner. Place him in the sitting position with the proper command. Then lift his front paws up until he is in a begging position. Hold him that way until he finds a comfortable balance and then let him balance himself. As he gets his balance, hold a piece of dog candy right over his nose. As soon as you let go of his front paws, lower the dog candy to his mouth and let him take it from your hands. Hold the dog candy firmly so it takes a few seconds for him to pry it loose, during this time you are saying BEG, over and over. From then on, you must bribe him with dog candy until he assumes the begging position upon the command BEG. Repeat the preliminary training until he eagerly goes into the begging position to earn dog candy.

TRAINING YOUR DOG TO RETRIEVE

Most dogs are born retrievers and their natural instinct is to chase something that moves. First go to a pet shop and pick out a rubber toy. Try a rubber ball, a rubber bone, anything that attracts your eye. They are all made of completely harmless rubber and are safe even if your dog chews them up.

Then take your dog outside and throw the toy a few feet. He will usually

To teach your dog to retrieve, start with a dumbbell or bone, saying "Fetch" while
he holds it, and "Give" to release it.

chase it and pick it up. If he doesn't, then you must walk him over to the toy and place it in his mouth and walk him back to your starting position with it. Repeat this operation until he learns the game. Once he goes after the toy, call him to you. If he drops it along the way merely send him back for it by pointing to the object. If necessary, walk him back to the toy, put it in his mouth and walk back with him to the original starting position. When he successfully brings back the object you can reward him with a piece of dog candy.

Two Orientals at ease: a stately Afghan and lordly Siamese; Afghans will get along well with other pets in your home.

7. Showing Your Afghan

As your puppy grows he will doubtless have many admirers among your friends, some of whom are bound to say, "Oh, what a handsome dog —you should certainly show him!" Perhaps even a breeder or judge will say he has show possibilities, and although you didn't buy him with that thought in mind, "Cinderella" champions do come along now and then— often enough to keep dog breeders perennially optimistic.

If you do have ideas of showing your dog, get the opinion of someone with experience first. With favorable criticism, go ahead making plans to show him. For the novice dog and handler, sanction shows are a good way to gain ring poise and experience. These are small shows often held by the local kennel club or breed specialty club, found in many cities. Entry fees are low and paid at the door, breeds and sexes are usually judged together, and the prizes and ribbons are not important. They provide a good opportunity to learn what goes on at a show, and to conquer ring nervousness. Matches are usually held during the evening or on a week-end afternoon, and you need stay only to be judged.

Before you go to a show your dog should be trained—to gait at a trot beside you, with head up and in a straight line. In the ring you will have to gait around the edge with other dogs and then individually up and down the center runner. In addition the dog must stand for examination by the judge, who will look at him closely and feel his head and body structure. He should be taught to stand squarely, hind feet slightly back, head up on the alert. He must hold the pose when you place his feet and show animation for a piece of boiled liver in your hand or a toy mouse thrown in front of you.

ADVANCE PREPARATION

The day before the benched point show, pack your kit. You will want to take a water dish and bottle of water for your dog (so that he won't be affected by a change in drinking water, and you won't have to go look for it). A chain or leash to fasten him to the bench, or stall, where he must remain during the show, and a show lead should be included, as well as grooming tools. The show lead is a thin nylon or cord collar and leash

Your Afghan needs exercise to be healthy, for he is naturally a swift-moving hunter. If you cannot let him run loose in fenced-in grounds, take him for a run in the park.

combined, which detracts from the dog's appearance less than a clumsier chain and lead. Also put in the identification ticket sent by the show super-intendent, noting the time you must be there and place where the show will be held, as well as time of judging.

If you have kept your dog's coat in good condition by weekly groom-ing, there is little to do the day before the show. Groom him thoroughly from the skin out again, and be particularly careful to work out mats, to clean the dog's teeth and if necessary wash his feet and legs if the dirt cannot be brushed out.

Entries close about two weeks in advance for the larger or "point" shows. You can obtain the dates of coming shows in your vicinity by writing to the Gaines Dog Research Center, 250 Park Ave., New York 17, N. Y. You will probably want to enter your dog in novice, or in puppy if he is between six and twelve months.

Don't feed your dog the morning of the show, or give him at most a light meal. He will be more comfortable in the car on the way, and will show more enthusiastically. When you arrive at the show grounds an official veterinarian will check your dog for health, and then you should find his bench and settle him there.

Take your dog to the exercise ring to relieve himself, and give him a final grooming, then wait at the ring for your class to be called. All male classes are first, in this order: puppy, novice, bred by exhibitor, American-bred, open.

The winners compete for Winners Dog, who is awarded points toward his championship according to the number present. The winner competes against the best female, then against champions entered in "specials only" for best of breed. The next step is the Hound group, where the best Afghan will compete against other hounds, including Beagles and Dachshunds, and the winner there goes on to try for best in show against Sporting, Working, Terrier, Toy and Non-Sporting winners.

Another aspect of dog shows is the obedience trial. Any purebred dog may compete, to be judged on performance, instead of conformation. There are three classes of increasing difficulty: novice, open and utility, leading to the degrees of C.D., C.D.X. and U.D.—companion dog (excellent) and utility dog. Tracking, or trailing, tests are also held.

If your dog has received the training we have described previously, he is well on the way to the necessary requirements for the novice class, and you may wish to continue. There are many obedience classes where an experienced trainer can help you with your dog; classes are held weekly at a nominal fee. It helps to accustom the dog to behaving in the company of others, but a daily training period at home is also necessary. For the novice class your dog must heel on and off leash, stand for examination, come when called and sit with you at the end of the ring for one minute, lying down for three minutes. In advanced trials retrieving, jumps, longer stays, and more difficult tasks are added. Attending an obedience class is excellent training for the show ring, or for a well-behaved dog you will be proud to own.